"I personally believe that *Selli*... concise and helpful for beginne...
—W...
Executive Vice President...
Wells Fargo Bank

"*Selling with Honor* is quick, thought-provoking and right on the money."
—Jon Douglas
Chairman of the Board
Prudential Jon Douglas
Company

"Practical, useful advice and real-world examples that will help anyone in business, young or experienced, enjoy their work and be more successful."
—Richard W. Rentzell
Account Team Director
Pharmacia & Upjohn

"Simple, direct and fun to read. An outstanding program for marketing and selling your product or service—especially for people who hate to sell."
—Jim Rosen
Founder and Chairman of
the Board
Fantastic Foods

(continued on next page)

"A privilege to read. Besides being informative (in a Mark Twain business-like way), it's entertaining and easy to follow. This book elevates the art of selling from Begging with Dishonor to *Selling with Honor*."

—Blair Ballard
Blair Ballard Architects

"Packed with tools and techniques that will improve your sales and your life."

—Thomas B. Hamilton
President
Flagship Mortgage Co.

"A guidebook for building and maintaining honest and profitable relationships in our knock-'em-down, drag-'em-out competitive world...Distills the essence of service and commitment in a way that applies as much to life as it does to business."

—Linda S. Bernstein
President
SeaSpace Corp.

"A terrific balance of inspiration and practical advice for succeeding in business while excelling at life."

—Bonnie Werchan
V.P. of Marketing
Lexi International

Selling with Honor

STRATEGIES FOR SELLING WITHOUT SELLING YOUR SOUL

LAWRENCE KOHN
& JOEL SALTZMAN

B

BERKLEY BOOKS, NEW YORK

This book is an original publication of The Berkley Publishing Group.

SELLING WITH HONOR

A Berkley Book / published by arrangement with
the authors

PRINTING HISTORY
Berkley trade paperback edition / April 1997

The Putnam Berkley World Wide Web site address is
http://www.berkley.com/berkley

ISBN: 0-425-15704-0

BERKLEY®
Berkley Books are published by The Berkley Publishing Group,
200 Madison Avenue, New York, New York 10016.
BERKLEY and the ''B'' design
are trademarks belonging to Berkley Publishing Corporation.

PRINTED IN THE UNITED STATES OF AMERICA

10 9 8 7 6 5 4 3 2 1

To my brother Robert,
for support and inspiration.
—L. K.

To my father,
who has always sold with honor.
—J. S.

"Try not to become a man of success
but rather try to become a man of value."
—ALBERT EINSTEIN

"Try being both."
—LAWRENCE KOHN & JOEL SALTZMAN

Contents

Introduction

When you first saw the title of this book you probably thought, *Selling with Honor*, isn't that an oxymoron?

To which we reply, "Not at all."

In *Selling with Honor* seminars, workshops and one-on-one coaching sessions, thousands of people have grappled with the question, "How can I effectively sell without selling my soul?"

The answer is now in your hands, transformed into a fast, easy read.

If you have to sell to succeed—and you do—we invite you to increase your sales, develop a better rapport with your clients and meet today's ethical concerns by *Selling with Honor*.

You'll do better in business . . . and in life.

—LOS ANGELES, CA
JANUARY 1997

Selling with Honor

PART ONE

Be Honorable

Honor the Buyer and the Seller

"Trust me," says the salesperson, "I won't steer you wrong."

Look out, we tell ourselves, *here comes the con.*

Paying lip service to being trustworthy or honorable has nothing to do with selling with honor. To sell with honor, you must behave in a way that feels comfortable and appropriate to both parties—that honors the buyer *and* the salesperson.

❧

"Honor the salesperson?" you ask. "What does that have to do with selling?"

Everything. Selling with honor begins when you can honestly say, "I have something of value to offer." Then all you have to do is communicate that value.

Know Your Value

Your first job is to communicate your value directly to yourself—to sell yourself on you. Otherwise, you face an uphill battle, asking yourself, *If I can't sell me, how can I sell anyone else?*

To overcome your anxiety about selling, you need to develop an unwavering faith in the value of your product or service.

❦

But what if I'm not convinced of my value?

Convince yourself. Most people hugely underestimate the value they bring to the table. Fearful of inflating their worth—overselling—they go the other way. Deflating their worth, they lead potential buyers to conclude, "You're right. Based on the limited value you've communicated, I really should go somewhere else."

Remember: To overcome your anxiety about selling, develop an unwavering faith in the value you offer.

"We only have 10 percent of the market, and that means that 90 percent of the women are buying the wrong cosmetics."
—Mary Kay Ash
    Founder, Mary Kay Cosmetics

Be Crystal Clear About What You Do

It's not enough to say, "I'm a good architect," or "I work hard for my clients." *Be specific.* Write down every benefit and service you provide. And don't stop writing until you have at least a page.

Next, ask trusted clients what benefits and services they think you provide.

Finally, based on client feedback, revise that original list of yours. Sing your praises as accurately and comprehensively as possible.

CASE IN POINT

An accountant reports, "It took me a long time to get the nerve to ask my clients for feedback. But when I started to hear what they had to say about me, and I saw their compliments in writing, I suddenly realized how much I did for them. Now I wonder if I'm not charging enough."

Write a Mission Statement

Borrow a page from corporate leaders like Johnson & Johnson and AT&T. Write a mission statement—a statement of the values or beliefs that will guide your selling behavior. In charting your rules for selling, pay particular attention to offering service, safety, guidance, and passion.

After writing your mission statement, revise it and keep revising it until your rules are stated as simply, clearly, and succinctly as possible.

$$\infty$$

But I don't know what my rules are.

Of course you do. Look to your own stories of selling success. Recall what actions you took to win the day and identify the underlying principles, or rules, you were following.

CASE IN POINT

At AT&T, corporate principles are spelled out in a one page document called Our Common Bond.
Regarding customer service, it reads, "We build enduring relationships by understanding and anticipating our customers' needs and by serving them better each time than the time before."
Now ask yourself this: If you were a salesperson for AT&T, would looking to principles like this—stated simply and clearly—help guide your selling efforts?
You bet they would.

If You Don't Like What You're Selling, Sell Something Else

Writing your mission statement will take time. But if the process causes you undue grief, there may be a very simple explanation: You may not like what you're selling.

When you do get business, you're resentful of the buyer—someone who's now forcing you to perform a service or sell a product you'd rather not be involved with. Ironically, you find yourself pitted against the buyer, in danger of acting abusively toward the very person who's paying the bill.

From the waiter who thinks his job is beneath him to the dentist who hates his practice, we've all been abused by people who did not want our business in the first place.

To sell with honor, honor what you're selling.

CASE IN POINT

After ten years of practice, a lawyer discovers he hates doing divorce work, a "gutter practice" he calls it, where the lawyers often make out better than their clients. Realizing he's unable to honorably sell himself as a divorce lawyer, he goes back to school and becomes a mediator—helping to resolve the same sorts of conflicts, but without all the cost, haranguing, and endless acrimony. And because he likes what he does for a living, he finds it a lot easier to promote himself.

PART TWO

Reach Out

Reach Out

We've all walked into a store only to be rushed by a salesperson who acts like he hasn't seen a customer all day. Overeager (and possibly desperate) he pushes to make the sale. And the more he pushes, the more you want to flee.

How do you avoid having to "push" to make the sale?

Reach out to the world. Increase your sphere of possible customers. The more you reach out to make contacts and friends, the less your odds of the desperate clutch. "Please, don't leave me. I've got to got to make this sale before you walk out the door and I'm left without a prospect in sight."

That's what makes some of those salespeople so pushy—pushing to close a deal for fear their next opportunity may be a long way off.

~⌘~

But aren't there people who have so much business they don't need to go out looking for more?

Absolutely. People who've met a large number of prospects have been successful at communicating their value. Now their phone's ringing off the hook and they've got more business than they can handle.

People in this position represent a tiny percentage of the everyday world. The rest of us—most of the world, in fact—still need to reach out daily to find more business.

Look, I'm just afraid that if I reach out for business, I might end up making a fool of myself.

Then we'll teach you to reach out appropriately, in a way that makes you—and your prospects—feel comfortable.

Make Friends

When it comes to business, personal contacts are key.

People do business with people they like.

Very often, people call on a particular business or service because they know and like the people involved. That's why they thought to call in the first place.
Remember:

People do business with people they like.

Get more people to know and like you, and more and more business will come your way.

☙❧

Isn't that somewhat cold and calculating, going out to make friends so you can turn them into business leads?

It's a fact of life. People who like us are potential clients, or people who can lead us to clients. That's how you've gotten a lot of your business already—through people you've met who took a liking to you.

All we're trying to do is help the process along.

"As a young lawyer on the make in 1984, John Sloss learned that independent film director John Sayles played in a weekly pickup basketball game at a high-school gym in New York City. Mr. Sloss showed up in sweats and, after a bruising game, made a point of chatting with Mr. Sayles.

"A decade later, that hustle has paid off . . . His marquee client [is] Mr. Sayles."

—From *The Wall Street Journal*,
March 31, 1995

Ask Questions

You've reached out and made new friends. Now you're ready to start selling. Right?

Wrong. Before you tell them what you have to offer, find out what they need. Otherwise, you risk acting inappropriately, reaching out in a way that will make you both feel uncomfortable.

Before you jump in with, "Here's what I can do for you," first find out what needs to be done.

ॐ

How do I find out what people really need?

Ask lots of questions and listen more than you talk.

CASE IN POINT

Black & Decker has a reputation for listening to consumers. In the 1970's, for example, the company discovered that consumers wanted a portable vacuum cleaner for smaller spills. This led Black & Decker to create the hugely successful Dustbuster.

In 1994, hearing that consumers wanted both hands free 75% of the time they use a flashlight, the company created the SnakeLight, a flashlight that can stand by itself or wrap around the wearer's neck.

How does Black & Decker stumble onto these innovative discoveries? They ask lots of questions and listen for needs.

> "Listening to your customers is a way to make a fortune."
> —Mo Siegel
> Founder, Celestial Seasonings

Know What You Do for a Living

When people ask, "What do you do?" very often they couldn't care less. It's a social convention, something to keep the conversation going. But it's also an opportunity to communicate your value.

Instead of simply saying, "I'm a lawyer," or "I sell computers," learn to convey how you *help* people, how you make their lives better. It's the difference between, "I'm a tax attorney," and "I'm a tax attorney. I help my clients save money by minimizing their taxes." One answer closes the door on conversation; the other opens it up.

Think of it as giving them a sound byte—a simple, memorable way of conveying the benefits you bring to your clients.

CASE IN POINT

In 1979, when General Electric was looking for a new advertising agency for its consumer products division, it held a competition between two finalists. Both agencies developed television campaigns that showed consumers enjoying various GE products. One agency used the tag line, "General Electric. Let us work for you." The other used the tag, "General Electric. We bring good things to life."

The winner?

The agency that showed how General Electric brings "good things to life"—a corporate pledge that's still being used.

When telling people what you do for a living or why they should hire you, the most powerful message you can deliver is, Working with me will make your life better.

"Our sales people don't necessarily sell products, they sell solutions."

—Arthur Blank
    Cofounder, The Home Depot

Learn That One Size Does Not Fit All

Be careful about that sound byte of yours.

As good as it may sound initially, don't wind up giving everyone you meet the same old line.

Learn to make telling people what you do for a living part of a give-and-take conversation, not a stand-up routine or an unsolicited infomercial.

CASE IN POINT

One day, a medical malpractice attorney finds himself saying: "I'm the David who fights the Goliaths of the medical industry."

He likes the line so much, he starts using it at every opportunity. At parties. Pitching new clients. When he meets a woman he'd like to ask out.

Unfortunately, he starts sounding like a TV pitchman, not the caring, devoted person he truly is. And his behavior starts pushing people away. What was once a spontaneous remark (just the right thing to say) becomes a slick, stale line.

Eventually, he senses there's a problem and returns to presenting himself as someone who's personable, caring, and likes to fight the good fight when he suspects malpractice. People start responding. And business picks up.

> "Be yourself, stay natural and dammit, smile once in a while!"
>
> —Lee Iacocca

Be Honest

Telemarketers face an awful challenge. In a single call, they need to establish a rapport, gain your trust, and make that sale. These demands lead some telemarketers to resort to desperate measures.

They'll glad hand you like mad, acting like your best friend in the world: "Dave, how are you today?" Or they'll tell your secretary, "I'm a new client. I'm sure your boss wants to speak with me."

Question: By reaching out to make new friends in order to get more business, aren't you being equally deceitful?

Not if you're honest; not if you disclose your intention to do business. By stating your reason for reaching out in the first place, you do away with the fear of manipulation: your fear you're manipulating them; and their fear they're being manipulated by one more salesperson posing as a friend.

❦

But it sounds so manipulative. All this trying to make friends just so I can sell them.

You're not trying to make friends, then trick them into being clients. You're trying to build relationships based on honesty. Get things out in the open. Disclose your intention to do business one day.

Just come out and say it? Be totally honest?

Try it sometime. Then watch them fall over.

CASE IN POINT

A businesswoman arranges for her husband and herself to have dinner with another couple, both of whom she'd like to win as clients. When the wine arrives, she toasts: "Here's to new friends." Her husband wants to crawl under the table ("I felt like I was in a beer commercial.") until his wife adds the words, "And if some business should come of it, so much the better."

Suddenly, says the husband, "I fell in love with her all over again, thinking, Who could resist a woman like this?"

Talk with Your Friends

When it comes to looking for business, friends are often overlooked.

For some, it's the unspoken fear that doing business with friends could jeopardize the relationship. "If you want to lose a friend," they'll advise, "loan him money or do business together."

For others, it's the concern that asking friends for business would reveal some flaw in their character. "They'll see me as needy or greedy."

For others, a more pragmatic concern: If I did business with friends, I'd have to give them a discount and better service.

Granted, there are risks. Would you take a group of people who know and like you and totally eliminate them as possible clients?

Remember:

People do business with people they like.

Think it over. Give it some good, honest thought and see if the idea of doing business with one or more friends gives you the willies or might just work.

Broach the subject with friends, and see how they feel about it. You might be surprised or have your worst fears confirmed. But you'll never find out unless you ask.

ॐ

Look, I've thought it over and it's out of the question. I won't take the risk of doing business with friends.

Okay, then how about asking your friends to refer you to friends of theirs?

What are they going to say? "Jerry's my friend. Why don't you hire him next time you need a contractor?" They don't know if I'm any good or not.

Fair enough. What if they said, "I don't know how good a contractor he is, but his house looks great. We've been friends for years, and he's a good, honest guy."

But why should they go out of their way like that?

They're your friends; they want you to do well. Besides, you're going to do the same for them.

PART THREE

First Give,
Then Receive

Stay in Touch

Every client you've ever landed has been the result of your marketing efforts—even if they were efforts you didn't know you were making.

We've all met someone socially or on the job and had a relationship develop over time. You stay in touch, become old friends, and eventually, keeping in touch with that person translates into business.

But unless that friendship evolves naturally, most people have no idea how to further the relationship.

For example: You asked for her business card and you really did mean to call. Then you stuffed it in a drawer somewhere, years went by, and she became a major honcho, president of Mega Industries. Now you're dying to call her, but you failed to stay in touch when you had the chance.

Stay in touch with the people you meet. They'll grow into friends over time.

Just remember: In business as in life, *it takes a long time to make old friends.*

CASE IN POINT

After five years with a large firm, a young architect decides to strike out on his own without a client in sight. Over the years, however, he's made friends with a lot of architects at the firm, including some partners. So he prepares for his departure by taking each of his architect friends out to lunch and telling them of his plans. Then he follows up by sending out announcements. Sure enough, they start sending him business.

There's only one problem. At the firm, he'd see his fellow architects on a daily basis. They'd work together, go to the same parties. But once he's out on his own, he fails to stay in touch. And little by little, referrals dry up.

Meanwhile, another architect also leaves the firm. And even though the second architect is junior to the first, he makes sure to stay in touch with his former co-workers. He drops by the office, sends bottles of wine to thank them for business, and remembers to treat them like the valuable friends they truly are.

Not only does he keep getting referrals, he hires two more architects to handle the load.

Make a Mailing List

Gather up those business cards you've been collecting and put them to use.

If you don't have a mailing list, it's time to make one; if you have a list, it's time to update it and put it to use.

Create a list of everyone you know who could possibly send you work. This is the first lesson in keeping in touch—knowing who, exactly, you'll be keeping in touch with.

If you find yourself resisting even the thought of such a list, don't be surprised. Creating your mailing list is like doing your taxes: It gives you a cold, hard look at where you stand—whether you're flush with friends or desperate for help.

But my mailing list would be so short. I've got less than a dozen contacts.

Join business organizations, chambers of commerce, community groups, any place you can think of where you can meet more prospects. And don't just send your dues in or buy a table at the annual banquet once a year. Go to meetings; get on committees. Reach out to meet a lot more people and start keeping in touch.

My mailing list is too long already. I have hundreds of people and half of them I haven't spoken to in years.

Then get on the phone and get back in touch.

But I'd feel so awkward about it, calling up people I've really lost touch with.

Would you feel comfortable calling up and saying, "I'm updating my mailing list, and I wanted to know if I could keep your name on it as someone to stay in touch with?"? That's an easy call to make.

For *you*, maybe.

CASE IN POINT

A management consultant at a large firm is asked to draw up a list of five former clients who she believes were satisfied with her work. But when it comes to calling them, she has a list of excuses: She's too busy; she didn't do that good a job; and besides, it was years ago.

Finally, she braces herself, picks up the phone, and calls the first person on the list.

"Why, Carol," says the former client. "You're just the person we could use right now!"

That one phone call sends shock waves through the firm. How, they all wonder, could a devout nonmarketer like Carol bring in a chunk of business worth $150,000?

Give Value in Advance

Lots of people talk about "added value," or throwing in something extra to sweeten the deal. But suppose you gave value in *advance* of the deal, giving value to your clients in advance of there being a business relationship.

Actually, it's done all the time.

When a lawyer gives free advice to a prospective client, that's value in advance.

When an investment firm sends out a monthly newsletter, that's also value in advance.

Or think of the enjoyment or value you get when you visit your local book chain emporium and spend some time in one of their very comfortable reading chairs. *Browse a while,* goes the message. *Make yourself comfortable. No one's pushing to make a sale.*

To sell with honor, give them value in advance.

Start serving your clients *before* they're your clients.

CASE IN POINT

A homeowner asks a gardener to take a look at his property and tell him how much he would charge to take care of it. While surveying the property, the gardener spots a sprinkler head surrounded by a puddle of water.

"Been like this for long?" asks the gardener.

"About a year."

With that, the gardener pulls out a screwdriver and has it fixed in a minute.

Having given the homeowner value in advance, he gets hired on the spot.

∞

How about business lunches? That seems like a tried-and-true form of value in advance.

True enough, but be careful: Many "tried-and-true" ways of doing business have, over time, become tired and trite.

Besides, look at the message you're sending: "Doing business with me means business as usual. If you're looking for someone who'll offer creative, innovative solutions, look somewhere else."

But it's not that easy to break from the mold.

You're right. It will take some brainstorming. But if you think hard enough, you just might come up with a winning solution.

CASE IN POINT

In New York City, a young commercial photographer is low on clients and even lower on cash. So there's no way he can afford to wine and dine potential clients. That's when he comes up with his creative solution.

He invites two dozen art directors—each a potential client—to a free Paul Simon concert in Central Park. He explains that he'll have his assistant stake out plenty of blanket space early in the morning, twelve hours before the concert starts. That gives his potential clients value in advance—terrific seats without the hassle of having to camp out all day. It also establishes the photographer as someone they can count on for creative solutions.

Today, that enterprising photographer has all the clients he needs, many dating back from the night he played host at a free concert in Central Park.

Before you go looking for that great idea they'll never forget, start with some business-as-usual approach and see if you can't come up with a slight variation. For example:

BUSINESS AS USUAL

- You take people to lunch, pick up the check, and hope they call you for business.
- You send out newsletters to everyone on your mailing list.
- You write articles for trade journals.
- At Christmas, you send out cards and gifts.

SLIGHT VARIATIONS

- Instead of taking your business prospects out to lunch one by one, take out a group—people in noncompeting businesses who could benefit by meeting one another. And make it a *creative* meal by taking them to an unusual restaurant.
- Supplement that newsletter with a free seminar in your area of expertise. Which doesn't mean you have to splurge for a hotel meeting room. Invite people to your office and have it catered.
- Be creative when identifying trade journals. Consider

the chiropractor who writes an article on carpal tunnel syndrome and gets it placed in the *Writers Guild Journal,* a magazine that's distributed to 10,000 television and film writers in the Los Angeles area, because they all do a lot of typing and many of them live within driving distance of his office.

- Avoid the Christmas rush; stay in touch throughout the year. Instead of sending those annual bouquets, for example, arrange with a florist to send special clients a *monthly* bouquet. Whatever the flowers, they'll be sure to serve as forget-me-nots.

Target

Years ago, there was a *Twilight Zone* episode about a sidewalk peddler with the uncanny ability to know exactly what certain people needed. The gifts he provided seemed fairly modest (spot remover, scissors, a train ticket to Scranton, Pennsylvania). Yet each turned out to be of major value to the receiving party.

When offering value in advance, your goal is much the same—to give each prospective client something of value that's just right for them. Though unlike the salesman in *The Twilight Zone*, you won't have to rely on magical powers. Having stayed in touch over time, you've learned about your prospects, and you have a sense of what they might need.

You've also taken the time to create a database on each prospective client: a running log on their business, family, everything you've learned about them to date. Now it's time to get specific, to target specific actions to meet their needs. Ask yourself, *"What can I do that will position me positively in the eyes of this particular prospect? And how can I keep giving value to the clients I have?"*

ॐ

What if I can't think of what to do for someone? Then what do I do?

Do nothing until you can think of an action that's right on target.

And if I still can't think of something?

Resist the urge to act prematurely. Keep in touch, keep learning about your prospect, and eventually you'll discover something that person needs you can easily provide.

It all sounds so calculating.

It is. So's trying to get a new job or romancing some-one you're attracted to. The more you calculate and plan things out, the better your chances for winning them over.

CASE IN POINT

On their second date, a suitor brings flowers for her and gift-wrapped bones for her Labrador retrievers. This guy's special, *she says to herself.* I've gotten lots of flowers before, but no one's thought to bring something for my dogs.

One year later, he pops the question and closes the deal.

Give Them Proof

David Letterman once took a *Late Night* video crew to visit half a dozen greasy spoons that all had signs promising World's Best Coffee. The joke, of course, was: how could *any* of them have the world's best coffee?

It's easy to say, "I'm the best in the world."

The issue is proof. What can you offer that proves your worth?

CASE IN POINT

Two computer consultants start their own firm, making sure to reach out and give lots of value in advance. They serve on panels where they offer free advice, meet reporters with whom they stay in touch over time, and wind up getting profiled and praised in a local business journal.

What they have now is proof—an independent source that says they're outstanding.

> "If I take a full-page ad in the *New York Times* to publicize a project, it might cost $40,000, and in any case, people tend to be skeptical about advertising. But if the *New York Times* writes an even moderately positive one-column story about one of my deals, it doesn't cost me anything, and it's worth a lot more than $40,000."
>
> —Donald Trump

Let Them Know You Have Their Best Interests at Heart

We've all been to some snooty salon or highbrow boutique where the hired help has treated us like dirt.

We're so great, goes the message, *it's more important to serve our needs than yours.*

Let people know you have their best interests at heart. Then you can guide and they'll be sure to follow, knowing you care about their needs, not just your own.

CASE IN POINT

A businesswoman trying out a new travel agent calls to book a flight weeks in advance, hoping to get a fourteen-day-in-advance discounted ticket. Unfortunately, she learns that all the discounted seats have already been sold or reserved. The travel agent suggests the following: "For now, let me reserve a seat at full fare. Then, when it's fourteen days before your flight, I'll call the airline to see if someone who's reserved a discounted ticket hasn't paid for it yet. If they haven't, the seat will be released, and I'll get it for you at the discounted price."

For the travel agent, the more expensive the ticket, the larger the commission. Yet his clever plan to try for a less expensive ticket proves to his caller: Not only am I resourceful, I have your best interests at heart.

Does our businesswoman wind up with a discounted ticket?

It hardly matters. What matters is she's so impressed, she dumps her old agent and switches to the new one.

Offer Guidance and Safety

At Joe Rombi's restaurant in Pacific Grove, California, our waiter introduces himself by saying: "My name is Horace. I'll be taking care of you tonight."

And he does.

When purchasing a product or service, what we want more than anything is guidance and safety: to be given the guidance to help make our choice, and to feel safe and secure once we do.

No one wants to place an order—for dinner or anything else—while living in fear it's the wrong choice and that disappointment lurks just ahead.

Guide, advise, and keep your clients from making dangerous mistakes.

CASE IN POINT

A young couple calls a childproofing company, Safer Baby, to come to their house to give them an estimate. The representative goes through their house room by room, pointing out potential problems and telling them about various products they can have installed. He tells them what's optional and what he considers a must. He also shows them a lot of things they can do on their own, like removing dry cleaner bags from clothes in their closet and putting away small odds and ends their baby could choke on.

During the hour or so, he demonstrates his caring to such a degree that when he hands them his estimate, they agree on the spot.

Having met someone who offered guidance and safety, there simply was no reason to look anywhere else.

Avoid the Beauty Contest

No phone calls.

Résumé only.

Play by our rules or don't play at all.

When someone else is giving the marching orders, it's tough to put your best foot forward.

Avoid the beauty contest. Don't stand around holding your breath while being compared to countless others.

But they're setting the rules? Yes and no. Regardless of their stated rules, there's an unspoken rule that always prevails: Value gets noticed.

CASE IN POINT

An infomercial producer is requested by fax to submit her résumé and demo reel to an entrepreneur with a new product to sell. Rather than simply play by the rules, she calls him up and discovers this will be his first experience with an infomercial.

What he really needs, the producer realizes, isn't a stack of demo reels but guidance and safety. Volunteering to meet with him, she provides value in advance by showing him how to avoid some common pitfalls and helping get him started in the right direction. And because she's shooting an infomercial at the time, she arranges to conduct their meeting at the production facility, where he watches her in action and gets further proof of her value.

The alternative, you'll recall, was signing up for that beauty contest—sending out her résumé and reel in hopes she'd be chosen Miss Infomercial Supplier.

"Don't get trapped in what is, look to 'what if?' "
—Allen Adamson
    Managing Director, Landor Associates

Be Charitable

Willie Sutton, when asked why he robbed banks, replied, "Because that's where the money is."

Same goes for charities. Charitable and philanthropic organizations are filled with wealthy, successful people who understand that charity not only helps others, it can also help them.

Give of yourself to a worthwhile cause. Get involved in planning and fund-raising. Prove to others the value of your work.

Rub shoulders with people who are doing good, and let some business rub off on you.

Isn't that social climbing? Trying to meet wealthy, influential people?

Like the politician running for office, trying to gather support with an expensive fund-raising dinner?

But isn't that working for the common good, not someone's own self-interest.

Why not both? Why not be charitable to the charity as well as yourself?

Serve the Community

Reach out to the community; give value in advance.

Remember those comfortable chairs at the book store? That's a great example of value in advance, providing comfort and a relaxing read well before customers spend any money.

These enterprising stores also reach out with the goal of becoming a community resource center, sponsoring events ranging from book readings and lectures to demonstrations like "Ten-Minute Meals" and "Thirty Minutes to a Painless Back." These events contribute to the community and bring customers and business into the store.

Reach out and serve the community. Learn to do well for yourself by doing good for others.

So it works for a bookstore. What do you do if you're selling hardware?

Offer free classes on basic home repairs. Or consider what Home Depot did. When parts of California were threatened by floods, Home Depot gave out 1,500 sandbags a day. They reached out, gave value in advance, and won the loyalty of consumers as well as free publicity. They got on local TV and radio, got written up in the Los Angeles Times, *even got mentioned on the network news. Publicity like that you just can't buy.*

Let's say you run a restaurant and you could use more business. Offer free cooking classes. Get written up in the local paper and get a new group of people to sample your food—people who'll get to know and like you, see your business as a value to the community, and return with their friends to share their discovery.

Whatever your product or service, think of a way to serve the community. Then let the community serve you in kind.

The Southern California Gas Company sends out its bills in envelopes marked "This Envelope Made From Recycled Telephone Directories." It's still a bill, and you're not eager to pay it, but you feel a little better about the company that sent it.

PART FOUR

See Yourself as
Others See You

Don't Beg

There's a word for what people do when they ask for business without demonstrating their value in advance: *begging*.

Begging tells people, "I can't take care of myself. Would you take care of me?"

In charity, we're more than willing to give to the needy, but in business, unless the person you're appealing to feels charitable or happens to be your brother-in-law, begging, as a sales technique, leaves much to be desired.

But you don't beg, you say? Think again.

Whenever you feel awkward about asking for business, chances are it's because you've failed to demonstrate your value in advance of your asking. So now what you're doing is begging for work. "C'mon, I can do it. Give me a shot."

"Why, are we related?"

Avoid the urge to beg for work. Instead, give them so much value and so much proof of your value, they'll beg you to work for them.

CASE IN POINT

A salesman, desperate to win an account, sends a photo of his children to a prospective client with a note that reads, "Please. Help me feed these kids."

"It was supposed to be a joke," he explains. "That's all it was. But the second I dropped that picture into the mailbox I began to worry. What if they thought I was serious? What if they really thought I was begging for work?

"Whatever they thought, it wasn't good. Not only did I never get work from them, they never returned another call."

Don't Be Desperate

No one wants to do business with someone who's desperate for the work. People want to do business with busy, successful, proven commodities—people, in fact, who don't need the work.

❧

But what if I really need the work?

Keep it to yourself.

Don't Ask Strangers for Money

Certain rules of behavior are genetically encoded. You can't avoid them, erase them, or pretend they're not there.

Like the rule that says: Don't give money to strangers. Which leads to the corollary: Don't *ask* strangers for money.

Why do people do business with people they know? So they won't have to give strangers money and strangers won't have to ask.

Don't be a stranger. Work to become a well-known, proven commodity, a reliable source they can take to the bank.

CASE IN POINT

A salesman tells the story of visiting a client when he gets a call from the hospital. His wife is in labor, and his car won't start. So he asks the client if he can borrow his car. The client agrees, and he makes it to the hospital in time for the delivery.

"What I learned," says the salesman, "is you have to develop such a level of trust they'd loan you their car if you asked. Now, that's a rule-of-thumb I use all the time: Unless I feel, This is someone who would trust me enough to loan me their car, I won't even think to ask for the business."

Be Passionate

Rather than begging, acting desperate, or asking strangers for money, learn to be passionate.

From Martin Luther King to Bruce Springsteen, passion is the spark that starts the fire, the magnet that draws people in.

When someone asks you, "What's up?" or "What's new?" reply with *enthusiasm*. "What's up? Let me tell you!" Tell them about that project you're working on, about the dream you have for its future success. Let them know you care about what you're doing and have the passion for your work.

People like to do business with people who like what they do. Share your passion and vision, and few can resist.

CASE IN POINT

Microsoft's Bill Gates, when asked if he were a good salesman, replied, "I'm good at sharing my excitement about where this industry is going and what we can do for a company."

Bill Gates's passion and enthusiasm has helped to make him the richest man in America.

> "You always have to have something you can tell people you're doing, something really nifty."
> —Leon Wieseltier
> Literary editor, *The New Republic*

See Yourself as Others See You

We've all seen movies where a character practices asking for a raise or a date in front of the mirror. Mostly, these scenes are played for comic effect, but the underlying concern is honest and real: *How do I appear to others?*

Take a look at the following adjectives and ask yourself which of these words people would use to describe your behavior? Would they say you were caring, creative, careful, cooperative, dedicated, diligent, ethical, fair, focused, forward-thinking, friendly, helpful, honest, imaginative, interesting, practical, reasonable, reliable, resourceful, respectful, persistent, patient, thorough, thoughtful, trustworthy and generally a nice person?

Or would they use words like impatient, rude, pushy, demanding, and unrealistic?

Starting with the adjectives above and adding any other words that come to mind, write out a list of adjectives under the heading: *This Is How Others See Me.*

Next, make a separate list of the attributes you'd like

to foster, the words you'd like people to use when describing your character. Use the heading: *This Is How I Wish They Would See Me*. Now comes the hard part. Assuming there's some discrepancy between the way you see yourself and the way you'd like to be seen, ask yourself, "What can I do to modify my behavior, to bring my wish list closer to reality?"

CASE IN POINT

The salesman confesses, "I was raised in a family where everyone told jokes. It was how you got attention, even love. So over the years—thinking I had to be funny to get people to pay attention to me—I wound up telling jokes all the time: The Willy Loman School of Selling.

"Then I made up those two lists of adjectives, and there was this huge difference between how I figured other people saw me, as a joke-teller, and how I saw myself, as an educator, as someone who could help his customers to improve their lives.

"So I decided to change, to make a concerted effort to communicate to the world: 'Here's the way I'd like you to think of me; here's the way I'd like to be known.'

"I still allowed myself to be funny, but I stopped telling jokes. And I slowly developed this new way of selling—being diligent, caring, and a lot of other words that came up on that wish list.

"I admit it. I was one of those guys who was always saying, 'Say, did you hear the one about the traveling salesman?' But after a while, it just wasn't me, and it sure wasn't helping to bring in the business."

> "Everybody likes a kidder, but nobody lends him money."
>
> —Willy Loman,
> *Death of a Salesman*

See Your Product or Service
as Others See It

A manufacturer of picture frames pastes their "Suggested Retail Price" sticker right on the glass—which is something you don't even think about until you get it home and find yourself struggling to pick, peel or scrape it off, hoping you don't scratch the glass or plastic in the process.

How could they do such a thing? you ask. *How could they be so incredibly inconsiderate?*

When offering your product or service, learn to see what you're selling from the buyer's perspective. That's step one.

Step two, of course, is doing something about it.

CASE IN POINT

Ikea furniture stores—mindful that a lot of customers bring their young children along—make shopping there a lot easier by offering free strollers, a changing room for babies, and a supervised Ballroom where their kids can play, leaving Mom and Dad to wander the store—and spend lots of money—without having to worry about keeping Junior out of trouble.

The lesson is simple: Having learned to see the shopping experience as their buyers see it, Ikea delivers exactly what's needed.

Take a Survey

There's a surefire method for finding out how your customers view your product or service: Take a survey.

Ask them: Are we being helpful? Are you happy with our work so far?

If the answer's Yes, you both feel better; if it's No, ask what you can do to make things right—so you can work to fix things before they go elsewhere.

Meanwhile, asking customers for their opinions strengthens the relationship and increases loyalty—because people like to be asked and feel like they're heard.

❦

I'm terrified of asking. What if they're unhappy?

When would you prefer finding out, when they're miserably unsatisfied and screaming divorce, or when there's still time to kiss and make up?

> Let the seller beware. Just because a customer doesn't make his feelings known doesn't mean he's happy. Surveys conducted by the Harvard School of Business consistently reveal: For every customer who stands up and complains, two others elect to not say a thing.

CASE IN POINT

A consultant who specializes in preventing workplace injuries gets his first big assignment: to create a three-day seminar for a major corporation. If he does well with this project, promises the head of personnel, she'll recommend him to their five branch offices.

Determined to wow them, he asks what they're looking for, designs a project they approve, and flies to Chicago where he gives it his all: three full days of lectures, videos and exercises for reducing fatigue. When the seminar's over, the head of personnel walks him to his car. "Mind if I make a constructive criticism?"

"Not at all."

"I've been very disappointed for the past three days. I was hoping for a lot more exercises."

The budding consultant wants to crawl under a rock. "I could have given you tons more exercises! All you had to do was tell me."

True enough.

Yet all the consultant had to do was take a survey, to ask his sponsor during a break, "Is this what you're looking for? Are you happy with what I'm giving you so far?"

For want of a survey the client (plus those five branch offices) was lost forever.

"If something's wrong, the question to ask is, 'What can I do to make it right?' Because customers always have something in their minds that would make it right."
—Aime Morgida
Regional vice president,
Whole Foods Market

Don't Kill the Messenger

In ancient Greece, when a messenger arrived with bad news, it was often the practice to kill him. As Sophocles himself observed, "Nobody likes the man who brings bad news."

Of course, we no longer take out a sword and assassinate the messenger, but that doesn't stop us from assassinating people's *character* when they don't approve of our product or service. "He doesn't like what I'm selling? The guy's an idiot!"

Because your prospect fails to value what you're selling, you turn around and devalue him. "That idiot. What does he know?"

Consider another approach. Rather than killing the messenger, what if you embraced him? What if you said to yourself, "I don't like what he has to say, but maybe I can learn from it. Maybe his negative comments can guide me to make a positive change."

It's always easy to kill the messenger; what's infinitely harder is to consider his news as something worth hearing.

CASE IN POINT

Let's go back to that consultant standing by his car with the head of personnel. When she delivers the bad news, "I've been very disappointed for the past three days," the man is crushed, defeated. Driving to the airport, all he can think is how much he hates her: The nerve of that woman, how could she abuse me like that? We agreed in advance to exactly what I'd do. Now she changes her mind but doesn't tell me about it until I'm three days dead. She's the one who caused the whole crisis!

It goes on like this all through the flight, until the plane descends to make its landing and the truth of the matter suddenly appears: She's not a terrible person, her opinion of what happened can't be dismissed. As much as I'd like to blame her for the problem, I have to accept responsibility. If I had stopped to ask, if I had taken a survey, I could have prevented this whole disaster.

In Chinese, the word for *crisis* and *opportunity* is the same. Whatever the crisis, work to turn it into a learning opportunity.

PART FIVE

Proceed with Caution

Be Patient

While cultivating your contacts, keep in mind that results can be long in coming.

Remember:

It takes a long time to make old friends.

Be patient, be careful, and be willing to wait.

Can't I skip a step, do something daring that wins them over?

For the buyer, it's "Strike one, you're out." Step on their toes just once, and you'll leave a more lasting impression than the fifty times you did them good. Better to proceed with caution—targeting actions and taking your time—than risk doing damage you can never repair.

"Be nice to everyone. Be polite. Serve one customer at a time."
—Dave Thomas
Founder, Wendy's Hamburgers

Look for Work When You Don't Have the Time

To avoid the temptation to "skip a step" or act inappropriately, start looking for work when you don't really need it.

When your plate is full, you'll find it's infinitely easier to communicate your value, presenting yourself as a busy, successful, proven commodity.

Now you're not begging, you're spreading good news.

❦

But what if I really need the work?

Unfortunately, this places you at a distinct disadvantage. Remember: People like to do business with people who don't need the work. And if you do need the work, it's not that easy to act like you don't. "Boy, am I doing great. It's my best year ever!"

"What are you working on?"

"Right now? Well, uh. You know, lots of stuff."

"Think you could be any less specific?"

"I don't think so, no."

Seek Out Your Peers

In theory, it's great to sell when you don't need the work; but in practice, there are plenty of times when you do need the work. That makes it tempting to do something rash.

When in doubt, seek out your peers—your personal board of advisors. Ask them, "If you were the client, how would you react if this is what I said or did? Would it make me a hero or a bum?" Talk things over. Heed their advice.

Before taking the chance of making a strategic blunder, try things out in a safe, nonthreatening environment, among people you know whose opinions you trust.

⊗⊗

If I asked for their help, I'm afraid people would see me as weak or indecisive.

Then choose someone who cares about you and cares enough to keep things confidential.

Go through every name on your mailing list and ask yourself, "Is this a person I could turn to for advice?" Or turn to a trade organization chat line. But do be judicious. Don't wear out their welcome mat with your Problem du Jour.

Start Small

To minimize danger, guide your buyer to starting small.

Rather than trying for the whole enchilada—and asking your buyer to make a huge leap of faith—create a plan that lets him "start small," giving you the chance to prove just how valuable you truly are.

Start small, prove your value, and let the relationship grow from there.

The owner of an older house finds Dalo Plumbers in the Yellow Pages and calls them to fix a leak. Dave and Tim show up, do the job for a reasonable price, and the homeowner's happy. Though they do advise her that the lead pipes in her forty-year-old house are showing their age and will have to be replaced—not today, but sooner or later.

Over the next few years, various plumbing needs arise at the house. Dave and Tim keep getting called and, from time to time, they gently remind their customer about those pipes that will need replacing.

Finally, one of those pipes starts to give, creating a leak that Dave and Tim are prepared to patch—until the homeowner says to them, "Maybe it's time to replace *the pipes. Wouldn't that be smarter?"*

It takes a few years to win the big one, but Dave and Tim get the job and get their price.

> According to a 1994 survey by Olsten Staffing Services, nearly 40 percent of temporary workers get offered full-time jobs. Having demonstrated their value with a small, safe deal (temporary employment), the buyer turns around and proposes more: "We're sold on you. How would you like to work full time?"

Tell the Truth

Aside from convicted felons, most people would say that car salespeople are the biggest liars in the world.

To help combat this impression, the National Automobile Dealers Association now sponsors seminars in ethics and etiquette, where salespeople learn that telling the truth is a smarter way to sell.

Don't lie, don't deceive, and don't overpromise. *Tell the truth.* What you sacrifice in immediate profit will be more than made up in referrals and repeat business.

CASE IN POINT

A potential client asks a lawyer if she's had any trial experience. She replies, "Contrary to what you see on TV, the last thing you want to do is go to trial: It's always a crap shoot and there's too much to lose. Even if you win, it's enormously expensive. So I win on my briefs, or we move to arbitration. And for fifteen years, that's exactly what I've done."

Tell the truth, no matter what. And if you can turn a negative into a positive, even better.

> "Don't hide even small defects. Always disclose something that would bother you, because it would also probably bother a potential buyer. And if they found out, they'd wonder what else you were hiding."
>
> —Pam Strauss
> Sales manager, Shorewood Realtors

Do What You Do,
Not What You Don't

You've started small, developed trust, and now your buyer wants a product or service that is outside your area of expertise.

You're tempted, really tempted, and even though it makes you a little nervous, you start thinking to yourself: *How tough could it be?*

Then you step outside your comfort zone and take the bait, only to discover that your clients request is a lot more challenging than you had imagined. Now you're at risk of disappointing, and possibly losing your trusting client.

Unless you're experienced and know the ropes, nothing in life is as easy as it looks.

Don't oversell. Only make promises you know you can keep.

CASE IN POINT

A homeowner asks a painter to give him a bid on painting the exterior of his house. At the same time, he asks the painter if he could also repair and reseal the deck.

"Sure," says the painter, thinking, How tough could a deck be? *He gives the homeowner bids for both jobs and the bids are accepted.*

The work on the house turns out great, but the work on the deck is riddled with problems. And because it takes a lot more time than the painter had figured, he turns in a bill for the deck that's double *the bid.*

He and the homeowner do not part as friends.

"Dell used to say, 'We're going to do everything.' . . . The hard thing is figuring out what you're not going to do."
  —Michael Dell
    President and founder, Dell Computers

"We don't sell pantyhose."
  —Van Butler
    Divisional vice president, Toys "R" Us

PART SIX

Plan to Succeed

Find Mentors

No one says you have to brave the frontier all by yourself.

Find mentors.

Seek the counsel of industry leaders and discover that people who've achieved great success often welcome the opportunity to help others do the same.

❦

Why would some big shot help someone like me?

Because lots of them got help from others.

Early in his career, Steven Spielberg connected with MCA Chief Executive Sidney Sheinberg, who helped young Steven make a film called Jaws. *Once established, Spielberg took a liking to a young director, Robert Zemeckis. Under Spielberg's tutelage Zemeckis went on to direct* Forrest Gump. *Now Zemeckis is helping others.*

Review your mailing list. Target someone you admire to lend a helping hand. Then find a way to give that person value in advance, even if means paying for guidance.

CASE IN POINT

A young criminal defense lawyer is having trouble getting referrals, so he hires a leading attorney to advise him on a trial. They get to know one another, become friends over time, and the novice attorney starts getting referrals from his former mentor.

Don't Only Sell to Buyers

Sell to people who can *refer* you to buyers. If you run a restaurant, court the favor of the concierge of a nearby hotel; if you're a photographer, make friends with a wedding planner; if you're a housepainter, build a relationship with a real estate agent, someone who can recommend you to their buyers as well as their sellers. (Just don't tell them you also do decks.)

CASE IN POINT

In the 1980s, with no money to advertise, family-run newcomer, Make-up Art Cosmetics (MAC), decides to target makeup artists in order to build a word-of-mouth reputation. Giving value in advance, the company offers makeup artists a 40 percent discount off prices that are already lower than the leading brands. Ten years later, MAC sales grow to more than $100 million a year, and the company gets purchased by industry giant Estée Lauder.

Turn Your Clients into Advocates

Word of mouth is the best advertising there is—and the cheapest. Imagine the thrill of someone calling to say, "Frank says you're great. When can we get started?"

Rather than sit and wait for these calls, help make them happen by turning your clients into advocates for your business.

First, consider asking clients for a letter of thanks, words of praise for a job well done. Putting their feelings down on paper strengthens the relationship, and asking for a letter lets them know you're open to the idea of getting their help in finding new business.

Next, see which clients you have who might feel comfortable making a strategic introduction, whether it's picking up the phone or taking you along to a trade organization meeting—a low-pressure setting for introducing you to potential clients.

Finally, ask yourself: "How can beating the drum for me benefit my client as well?"

CASE IN POINT

When MCI first devised their Friends & Family plan, they hit upon what looked like a terrific idea: Get customers to give them the names and numbers of up to twelve friends and family members so everyone in their "Calling Circle" can get a discount when calling one another—as long as they're currently using MCI or they switch to MCI.

It was an ingenious plan. By getting customers to serve as referral sources for MCI, not only do they benefit, but their friends and family benefit as well.

What the company discovered, however, was that a lot of people didn't like hearing that a friend or relative supplied their name and phone number without their knowledge.

Eventually, MCI modified their marketing. Now they no longer ask for a list of names in order to make unsolicited calls.

When asking for a referral, get your client to make the first call. Anything less and you could be a nuisance.

Send Letters of Thanks

Whenever someone tries to send you business, be sure to send a letter of thanks.

It's easy to make a phone call or leave a message on voice mail. A letter of thanks says you care enough to take the time to write, and a handwritten note says you really care.

Whether or not you get the business, your letter of thanks will serve you well—as value in advance of their next referral.

❦

So, I should thank them even if I don't get the business?

You're not thanking them for the business; you're thanking them for the effort they made on your behalf. Otherwise, you're sending the message, "If you're successful, I'll show my gratitude; if not, I can't be bothered."

CASE IN POINT

An advertising executive offers to help an aspiring copywriter by introducing him to the creative head of his agency. The writer gets to show off his portfolio but fails to get a job offer. He also fails to thank the executive who set things up, who reports, "I went out of my way for this guy and that was the last I ever heard from him. As for the creative head—even though he got nothing out of it—he thanked me in writing for bringing him a possible hire. It took him all of five minutes and made a major impression."

Never Make a Phone Call Without a Plan

Making a phone call without a plan is like getting in the car with no idea of where you're headed or how you'll get there.

You never want to call just to say hi.

You want to target your call before you make it. Decide ahead of time exactly why you're calling, and know what actions you'll take to achieve your goal.

If They Won't Return Your Calls, Write a Letter Instead

Letter-writing is the art of precision. Better than a well-targeted phone call, a letter gives you the opportunity to get your message across with pinpoint accuracy—as long as you're willing to write it, revise it, and revise it again.

A word of caution: Try not to send out your letter until the next morning. Seeing what you've written after time has elapsed can save you from sending a message you may later regret.

Be Persistent

What happens when a prospect says No?
Some of us hear No, others, Not yet.
The issue is persistence.

CASE IN POINT

Starting in 1967, engineer and inventor Allen Breed tries to sell air-bag sensors to Detroit automakers. But the Big Three want no part of this new and expensive technology, and they keep saying No until an act of Congress forces their hand in 1984.

In 1995, nearly thirty years after Breed's first rejection, Breed Technologies sells 23 million air-bag sensors for a net profit of $110 million.

Looking back on the old days, Breed recalls, "We lost track of how many times we heard No."

"I lose most of the time. For me, losing is just learning how to win."

—Ted Turner

"It's not whether you get knocked down. It's whether you get up again."

—Vince Lombardi

Know When to Quit

You've been patient and persistent and given them value in advance. Now they won't return your phone calls, and your letters go unanswered.

Despite your best efforts, certain prospects may never pan out, which brings us back to where we started:

Honor the buyer and the seller.

At the point when it starts to feel abusive—and you fear becoming abusive yourself—it's time to pack up the tent and call it quits.